S0-BBD-420

R01080 41093

stone floods

CHICAGO PUBLIC LIBRARY
BEVERLY BRANCH
1962 W. 95th STREET
CHICAGO, IL   60643

This book is for
Nora
my durable dam

Trevor Joyce

stone floods

New Writers' Press
Dublin

61 Clarence Mangan Road,
Dublin 8.
Tel. 4541906

© Trevor Joyce 1995

Cold Snap, Cold Course, The Turlough, and Cry Help have been
previously published in The Irish Review
Coumeenole has appeared in Pathfinder, Ed. Michael Smith,
published by The Educational Company, 1994

•

Publication of this volume has been made possible through the
generosity of George Hitching, and of Tom Smith, of the Castle
Lounge, Dublin

ISBN 0 905582 01 2

R01080 41093

Table of Contents

CHICAGO PUBLIC LIBRARY
BEVERLY BRANCH
1962 W. 95th STREET
CHICAGO, IL   60643

Dragons and fish see water as a palace, and it's just like human beings seeing a palace. They don't know it flows. If someone says "this palace you see is running water," the dragons and fish will be astonished, the way we are when we hear that "mountains flow". Still, there may be some dragons and fish who understand that the columns and pillars of palaces and pavilions are flowing water.

Dogen, **Mountains and Waters Sutra**

Rocks turn to rivers, rivers turn to men.
Herrick

The Opening
for P.C.

You are reading this book
On the table are letters a mirror some flowers
from which a leaf falls down
Behind is a wall in which there is no door
but you have opened it
and gone through

You hear these words
Your shadow moves across some photographs a leaf the threshold
which is badly worn
Beneath is the floor in which there is no chasm
yet you have stumbled
and dropped through

I have shut the book
and there is silence here
Now by the window
I look to the night
which has begun to fall
which will not be long now

1983

Fast Rivers

for Michael Smith

right at the very
instant of delivery
  the messengers
begin to fail
and are already
  exhausted

when we see the moment so
instantaneously
  spent
reckoning surely we regard
time not yet come
  extinct
let not the fool delude himself
that which he foresees
  will last
no longer than the bygone show
and all things thus
  shall pass

our lives are fast rivers soon
delivered to the sea
  of death
whereto go all dominions down
exhausted and
  are quenched
there must find the slightest rill
with tributary stream
  and flood
all then levelled utterly
daylabourer
  and lord

this world is but a road to one
wherein is no abiding
  grief
he needs due bearing who would not
from that true path
  fall off
the setting out is at our birth
we travel as we live
  dying
at last complete the course
and in that death
  lie down

The Turlough
for Celestine

It is raining elsewhere

Vertical rivers reverse
stone floods
the karst domain
each sink turns source

Rock brings forth fruit elsewhere

The action of the clock
runs down
through fissured hours
wells up lost time

All is not lost elsewhere

The emigrant returns
old loves
reach out their arms
gold leaves fly up

Time heals all wounds elsewhere

Bullet returns fire from flesh
to gun
the dried stain weeps
bone knits again

No mark gets the cold deck elsewhere

Boxed by his court of spades
Jack wakes
from his stone watch
that springs each arch

London Bridge is falling down elsewhere

Circuits and gates collapse
in sand
the face the glass
composed breaks down

Raw head finds bloody bones elsewhere

Vast hands stop at the stretch
knuckle
of blazing gas
and wrist of stars

The gods explode this turn elsewhere

Red giant and white dwarf
come in
in a blue shift
Venus meets Mars

There is thunder now elsewhere

Under an incandescent sky
flash floods
spread out this lake
is on no map

Strands

for P.C.

I have come indoors
Nothing moves outside
but the sea
in these drowned valleys
disassembling its past

If there is dark fruit forming
the roots will run deep in this rich earth
the growing timbers branch
through your night dreams

I have shut the door
The air outside is harsh
where the sea
broadcasts sharp seed
over a moon of salt

If there are metals ripening
that corn will bend to this slow storm
that new bread rise
through your unrecognized intents

I have opened this book
because elsewhere
there is only the sigh
of tall cliffs shod with sand
walking into the sea

If there are things intended
those strands will reach beyond this time
those vestiges extend
through your disquietude

Uncertain fingers now dissect
from the transformed wave
stone fish
They spin and sink
The sand receives them

Verses with a Refrain from a Solicitor's Letter
for George Hitching

As when a faded lock of woman's hair shall cause a man to cut his throat in a bedroom at five o'clock in the morning; or when Albany resounds with legislation, but a little henpecked judge in a dusty office at Herkimer or Johnstown sadly writes across the page the word 'unconstitutional' – the glory of the Capitol has faded.

Benj. Paul Blood

Dear Sir, I was this morning straight
after the news and forecast
hanging from an old appletree in my garden
a small Japanese bell
when I received through the post your importunate
and quite misguided threats

and in this regard time shall be made of the essence

An injunction, you say. An obstruction,
you say. You've a lot of chat for someone
that's not even clear who he's talking to.
Does this help: not only have I
not erected any obstruction
in the form of a barbed wire fence or otherwise

and in this regard time shall be made of the essence

but I'm attempting today to rest and recover
from the effects of an obstruction in my own passages?
I have, it pains me to have to spit it out, a strangury,
and you've got the wrong man, chief,
I've better blockages to worry about
than the one at the back of some godforsaken hotel in Midleton

and in this regard time shall be made of the essence

What's more, my bell is mute.
The inscribed slip that made its tongue
chime in the wind, flew off. It's not my day.
Far from putting up barbed wire fences,
I'd prefer, right now, to see one of those bright Byzantine
Christs come striding across from the opposite hills

and in this regard time shall be made of the essence

fresh from baptizing Adam, vast and very masterful,
lugging a patriarch along with each arm no doubt
from some new-harrowed hell
and scattering from his feet a fine debris
of locks, bolts, spancels, cuffs, gyves, fetters, stocks,
and other miscellaneous hindrances

and in this regard time shall be made of the essence

And what would our Neighbourhood Watch do then?
Put the polis on his tail, stay home, and watch that hooligan
as he'd come, breaking contracts, flattening fences
and leaving gates and prisons open behind him.
Yes, he's the man would soon break down
the calculus that stopped my flow

and in this regard time shall be made of the essence

And not like a thief in the night,
but openly I'd have him
eliminate all limitations,
peel walls and roofs away like rind
and with his knife of stars
reveal what soft exotic fruit grew ripe within

and in this regard time shall be made of the essence

unchain Prometheus from his rock
to stretch and scratch at last and fire
stones at that bloody bird,
allow Eurydice ascend
to feel the strange dew fall
chill through her faded dress

and in this regard time shall be made of the essence

remove the ratchet from the clock, North
from the needle, run the many down to one. (Oh no,
hold on there, God, we can't have that!
I won't be one with our friend the illicit
erector of barbed wire barricades,
or this damned notary. Cut!)

and in this regard time shall be made of the essence

It's evening now. The bell's transformed.
With a laurel leaf lashed to its tongue
it cries out clear in the wind.
I'll just sit tight till the Ipral sets me up
and I no longer pass blood,
or feel weak when I attempt to stand

and in this regard time shall be made of the essence

take idle note of that shrill song:
past flight and hot pursuit
terror passing cold restraint to come
then when I'm up to it again, forgetfully,
turn that stock still.
I trust this terminates our correspondence, Sir

and in this regard time shall be made of the essence

Cold Snap

Hammers of ice strike through the chiming earth.
Quartz and felspar writhe and tear. Oppressed
by frost the glistening mica weeps, while mineral
centuries shatter and sift to a quick sand.

Watch the high pines glint on a coal ground
and the windfall stonefruit wait.
Wrenbones fake iguanodon, invert the fossil
record into air. Among these simultaneous ages

houseless, desolate, dark forms slide,
(glazed the clear dew of their gaze)
observe it is a bitter season, that it cannot
last. But if there be anywhere some heat

it is remote. Through such white measures heart in mouth
we pass, fearful of landslips, tremors,
or the seismic shock would fault the brittle
light. Wordbreath ghosts these galleries.

Lines in Fall

I
Bag of bones cant lie down
to night
timbers settling
crack them up right
under Orrery Hill

head waters run bone dry
springs stop
fall rains fill up
resurgent courses
where the flood divides

the fabric all washed up
gives way
to thread bare ribs
remnant the wave un
weaves in ropes of sand

the loose ends ravel out
until
the form breaks down
its raw material
and nothing else survives

this cataract cuts off
all lines
into the past
the old tissue far
too slight to stand that fall

II
the face turns
stone ground
in the fall moon
cold peregrine in transit
fret to bits

where a hard
rain picks
this dream to shreds
a sharp wind in the easts grip
combs bones straight

that head long
home ward
warp from the well
dressed frame falls as the sand sifts
down silts up

groundless fears
stop then
now that yarns spun
out the flocks blown far afield
from tenters

bare ruined wires
run way
beyond these lines
night weaves new cloth the moon
her shuttle

Parting Words

If there's going to be a general resurrection
count me out

I wouldn't want that over again
not even the good bits

repetition would sour them
the rancid cud sicken me

but if in the final assembly
some indefatigable godhead twists my arm
then purged of memory

I'll take the part of water
reaching down through the lodged earth

or light exact oblique
at the delicate junctures

or a hand touching
and touching and touching

Ballyferriter, 2 June '91
Shanakiel, 30 June '92

Cold Course

The jaded sun lies low in his halt galaxy,
set hard like honey in the stiff comb,
with house and planet, tree and shivering peregrine,
all subjects under him consepulchred,
underfoot and done for, a mere smoke of stars.
The August heat, geometry of dance, full wilt
and fall: all yet survive in the slow sugars;
so, he now sits throned in dust, holds
vestiges and memoranda for his court,
whose armies dominate their night
quicksilver courses irrigate.
These he thought measures to kill time and grief.
Gorged on vermilion, his peers sweated
bright death, transfused the rockveins to their own.
The sovereign they bolted down still circulates
through this enchanted fastness of white sudden stone.

Coumeenole
for Owen

Dig! you cried

We dug out great trenches
and extended the abyss
down into an utter darkness
that stopped the heart with its cold

We fought off monstrous beasts
that nudged and butted us with their blunt heads
and from those regions of terror we brought back
massive rocks and curious shells

We threw up huge walls
and ramparts to repel
the encroaching forces
of chaos and disorder

We took all the boulders and all the sand
in the world and ranged up
mountains into the clouds
against the combing winds and the hard sea

And in the territories we had created
we established order
we set up high towers rivetted with light
and we built roads castles and cities

At evening as we left
looked back and saw whole continents dissolve
under the flood and heard
the soft collapse of walls and boundaries

you cried

Tocharian Music

for Máire Herbert

In these mountains there is a stream which flows away drop by drop, producing a sound as of music; once a year, at a certain date, these sounds are collected and made into a musical tune.

Wu K'ung

Still the jade woman circulates the cup
its empty now

Too long interbred with dragons
they grew restive
and rebelled
against the imperial mandate

Eleven thousand
died in the reprisal
and the city laid waste
the airs dispersed
only the names survive

Time slipped out of their tablature
and without stopping
fled
fugitive amongst those sands

Cry Help
for Brian Coffey

Cry help? You'll find me fast in my grave first
Who now could come if I did call
since our stronghold our hope our legitimate lord
has himself suffered seizure and failed?

Spun by the rip my mainstay snapped
arse breached with shit bile eats my gut
to see our ground our shelter our wildness our civilized precincts
hocked for a pittance by wasters

Our rivers their frets and divisions stand still
black marshes and palace the Bride and the Boyne
lake sound run red and the ominous seas
since that jack took the tricks from our king

Keen rain
on the road unsettles me
no sound comes near but the roar
of that unstoppable falls

Proud master of salient and hollow of royal demesnes
his stomach is lost with his lands
now the hawk who holds fast those rents and accounts
knows no man as kin

Come down too far from original heights
temporal races fret rockface
where raging headsprings supplement
the river that drops through the settlements

I stop and Death rides up to me
and the dragons are quenched in their courses
and I'm bound to follow my leader down
where His white ledger covers all the deal

Chimaera

for Tina Murphy

Ceres and Bacchus bid good night
sharp frosty fingers all your flowers have topped
and what scythes spared winds shave off quite

    a moth bred out of moonlight I disturbed
    from the dark folds where it lay hid

        a naked thing that seems no man may cheat
        and love like any jack
        another dressed may prove a beast

    that creature fluttered free but voided in my lap
    a maggot with a human head monstrous misshapen

such whose white satin upper coat of skin
cut upon velvet rich incarnadin
has yet a body and of flesh within

        whereas anything with six foot of skeleton
        with hands that grip with scalp of hair
        front teeth concealed inside a face
        and which leans forward as it runs
        is called a man with us

the joys of earth and air are thine entire
that with thy feet and wings dost hop and fly

    the sky unrolled its folds of purple and blue to the winds
    and later from these steps I saw on the horizon
    a village torched by soldiers blaze like a comet in the sky

then ah the sickle golden ears are cropped
dropping December shall come weeping in

the blood of horses become jack o lantern
the blood of men become will o the wisp
kites become sparrow hawks and those hawks cuckoos

when the sun opened its golden lashes on the chaos of worlds
and the earth was adrift with its cargo of ashes and bones
my terrified soul then fled through the grey web of halflight
but that spawn hung on in this shrill rush
and spun himself into the full of its white mane

cuckoos in due course again turn raptor
swallows become oysters seashells hatch geese

poor verdant fool and now green ice thy joys
large and as lasting as thy perch of grass
bid us lay in gainst winter rain and poise

apes grown of sheep fish that are rotten fruit
flies born of roe such transformations are

souls of the dead like mountain oaks uprooted by demons
souls of the dead like meadow flowers gathered by angels
sun sky earth man all had begun all gone

I cannot tell who loves the skelcton
of a poor marmoset naught but bone bone

Courting Trouble

Though I'm gone dog
tired tonight and sick
to the back

teeth of inventories and their
infernal
movements

of clearing accounts
and stocks and bonds
and switches

at the top
I yet must now attend
to still another bitter

letter from the law
which slow
and ravenous

gizzard
I'll survive to spike
since it wasn't for nothing

my durable dam
gristled me up
on greens and zest

I'll just
have a hot
bath soon

and make myself
some chicken
stuffed

with sage then pulse
and rice al dente
some fresh

salad on the side
and let those deadbeat
pigeons go

on grinding
uncomfortably
on their stools

21 June '93

Aperture

I took some photographs of Gougane Barra during a cloudburst
on the last day of February 1992, and hung the prints on the wall
of my lodging

sixteen months ago
swollen February
overspilled

into an extra day
the skies opened
bridges arched

under water
over head
cliffs drifted

blurred
by the dense
rain

falling
in the kitchen
still

behind scalding
clouds from the iron
I regret too fast

a shutter
for the insufficient
light flattens

the whole field

June 1993

Section

The heart,
fountain of desire,
vanishes.

        Lorca

In such estates
the child achieves
the mothers aim
whose hands knit dust

down streets of bone
what fathers terror
still runs on
whose eyes count clay

one inch of blood
an epoch of desire
each syllable
immeasurable grief

these intersect
those scarlet boulevards
the glimmering gods
ride down to us

Tohu-bohu

for Clare and Tom

I

First things first. One time a friend of mine came in for a few empty crates from a Mazda import agency. With a couple of rolls of felt he transformed his poky yard into a well-appointed loft where he kept fantails first and pouters, then tumblers, and finally some serious racing birds. At that juncture the fancy breeds had to go because their freaks disturbed the steady fliers. But he never banded his soft birds for racing, or bothered with the mandatory clock, just released them when he rose and let them settle back at evening to roost reassuringly secure. In the end though he got thoroughly sick of their ceaseless moaning, so he kicked out the lot of them, refitted the wire grilles with glass, sanded, sealed, and papered down the primitive walls, screeded the floor, and later on moved in himself, the family, and all their traps. For a good week after in these novel quarters he picked over an odd volume of Pliny's *Natural History*, shaken intermittently by the indignant refugees beating like stormy rain against the panes, and on the flat felt roof. This is a true story.

II

. . . do not look upon me on the dung-heap
nor go and leave me cast out
and you will find me in the kingdoms.
And do not look upon me when I am cast out among those who
are disgraced and in the least places,
nor laugh at me.
And do not cast me out among those who are slain in violence.
But I, I am compassionate and I am cruel.

Thunder Perfect Mind

When the shattering
key turns clockwise
the golden tumblers fall

through courts
where suits
are duly packed and paid

the ward turns
from the crooked talon
lofty strut and pinion

down their powers
and dominations
to the striking jack

III

And now these carriers
wheel painfully aloft
ringed round with tokens

protocols addresses
codes conventions empty forms
and the streams freeze in their shadow

remorselessly they brood
on every post
spill milk

and thick saltpetre
as they flap
from the twisted pair

to coax
all the news
comes down

so tell me
how would you put down
a lingering infestation

of goddamned angels?
set snares of blood
raise ghosts

and memories
for decoys
bait deadfalls

with true sleep?
or keep by the fire
a niptic cat

to stalk high winds
and pounce
on fallen stars?

they just don't get
the message yet!
suggestions please

so I can get
forever shut
of their close breath

fat with clay
stone floods
the midnight crashing

of their verminous wings

'93/4

In the closing days of 1993 my library and other traps were delivered
to my new lodgings near Kilcrea, Co. Cork

I've got no means of knowing for sure
if you can hear the knocking of the bells
as you anticipated from your open door
or just the slight hiss of the rain as here

this low cover that confounds all clarity
blocks from you too the hunter and the hounds
coursing in vain the high frost
from the zenith past this pitch past me

unthinking since at six I left you I've traversed
one entire quadrant of the sky
Algol ever duplicitous
salted your mine with stars as she swung by

since no-one's fixed your street-light there
that shorted in the recent storms
it's way too chancy now to call
the corner phone hoping you'd hear

but do my dear friend remember
to feed the fire I built
to counteract the streaming flood
inside your walls the spreading rot

here as the year turns over
anxious and half-insensible
with too much solitary alcohol
I stoke my own fire up

just a little on from that hard school
where dull O'Laoghaire learns at length
without either civility or song
the full weight of the heavy earth

I rise at intervals to welcome one
by one my new arrivals in
on boards of smooth white deal
for your pleasure I arrange

Dickinson and Dogen
Lorca and T'ao Ch'ien
with other esoterica
and miscellaneous pots and pans

my telescope leans blind against the wall
its mirror cataracted with fresh dust
lens unadjusted from the cloudy moon
we renounced last night

to set at large
the confined hour when hand
of thigh belly of head
make good sense unforeseen

now for a spell
the dead-headed
demon's carried
below the pole

it's high time to play again
with this present you devised
with care locate
your traces in the volatile oils

rosewood lavender and ceaseless
rosemary release their essential
and complex vapours
above the steady flame

that in the column of the lamp
burns almost enclosed
aware the unfinished buddha
at the shut summit

of the terraced worlds
sees the rough suns tumble out
where the furious high god
hurls his net

and each jewelled node
glitters with every other
as they fall
effortless exactly

through the empty now
let's together each
again make free
for the time being

that is not nothing

Owning

What bird was that obliterated
with its heavy wing the sun?

A legion of dust force marched
across the solitary wind
invades me

I could have spoken
with the narrow bone of your forearm
but I neglectful slept
just slept through grains and aeons
hand foot yard chain seconds seasons terms

Why do vain dust and the darkened bone
wrestle still for their place by the wall?

When the white stone flutters
in the intense heat
the river purrs in its night apart

I might have ravelled knotted time
out of your hair that goes on growing
into the night and hurts at dawn

I might have brought you water
to wash clear the blood from your lengthening nails
but I watched the high crop thorned with frost
quick courses clot locks close
on those whose property
is to be possessed at last

The Course of Nature

If heaven too had passions even heaven would grow old
Li Ho

Poor angels their high regard
fixed beyond the outer
horizon of stars

with tranquil fascination
watch the generation
and destruction of worlds

their urgent stride
shatters the capitals
of empires their serene

breath and thunderous wings
blast continents and seas
until sometimes randomly

distracted by the stray
falling of a small songbird
the delicate drift of white

ash inside a furnace
their eyes clouded
with unbearable pain and weariness

oblivious of their feet
bleeding from flints
vast wings moulting

and raw with neglect
newly they survey
all the tiny and discrete

effects of the world
and weeping to witness
such quick and irreversible decay

they stoop to gather them
into eternity and so
become the prey of immense

cats that sniff them
out to maul and play
fully dismember as they dine

on the rare giblets
of felled seraphs
and their squab

Golden Master

Time will lay
His yellow hand upon my photograph
Hernández
(Tr. Michael Smith; early draft)

I suspect that he can have
at most a rudimentary
awareness of his own situation
occasional nightmares

which he recognizes as such on waking
of a day when his hunger
and thirst may by no means be satisfied
when wine will stand

in a still cataract
poised between jug and lip
gilding his parched tongue
bread crumble in irregular grains

between his teeth
green apples ripen
most unpleasantly
the arm he grips the mouth

he'd kiss become arthritic bullion
and he must seek the quick river out
and wash and wash unceasingly
until it rinses off all trace

of this divine gift
down into its glittering silt
its rich alluvium

but now I flinch from him
as he stumbles through my house
a touching venerable figure
transmuting every chance exposure

each stray print
into the dearly treasured
eliminating all foreign
matter all admixtures

of other elements
as base impurities
as the embalmer with his metal hook
jabbed up through the left nostril

burst into the cranial cavity
reduced the brain extracted it
alongside heart and lungs
and other such soft offal

before elaborating
with his naphtha and his scented oils
the hardy flesh dressed up
for entry to eternity and night

Hearsay

for Mike and Irene

Deep deep below
the Norman tower
in one chamber
on twin trestles
lie two coffins
both evidently
of recent manufacture

These contain
the mortal remains
of certain patriotic brothers
executed by decapitation
two hundred years ago
for revolutionary treason
against a government
whose authority they rejected

On the wall
a brittle wreath
is suspended
from a nail

The chamber is otherwise
quite empty
of all but an ubiquitous
pervasive dust

The official guide explains
that for many years
the bodies lay exposed here
their upright heads

set alongside their feet
the solemn demeanour
of their parallel trunks
the otherworldly gaze
of each displaced face
all perfectly preserved
in the remarkable atmosphere
of this parched cellarage
until one day to celebrate
some obscure anniversary
an unknown reverential lady
brought in homage
into this grey place of sand
a wreath of fresh flowers

It was not for several days however
so the guide avers
that his attentive avatar
for this all happened
many years before
began to nose
an unprecedented fragrance
in the desiccated air
and presently observed
the obdurate brows
begin to melt
from the fixed fraternal frowns
and those thirsty bodies
of the long stiff brothers
drinking the freshness
of a distant garden
begin at last
to unbend together

till things soon got out of hand
as nothing could avert
their total relaxation
and their mixing grew unsocial

So they coffined them quick
to stop them making
an utter disgrace of themselves
and there they lie now
neatly boxed
till judgement day

Two closed
and shiny coffins
make a dull spectacle
scarcely worth
the cost of admission
but a Franciscan father I knew
once told me
the true story

One night it seems
a local woman
of unimpeachable veracity
whose confessor he was
called to the friary
and respectfully requested
an audience with him
which being granted
she pressed into his hand
a large brown paper bag
and said himself had been out
drinking with the lads
and got a bit carried away

and could Father
please set things straight again
whereupon she hurriedly left
and in the brown paper bag he held
his fingers found
an unexpectedly horny head
which on the following day
he faithfully returned
to the nearby rectory
to find his honest explanations met
with stony disbelief although
he being a fellow man
albeit of different cloth
no undue fuss was made

He claimed it was as a direct result
of such midnight gallivanting
that the stiff boys
straight were boxed

My guide cannot be shaken though
from his mandated history
and when I question him
imperiously points
to the dry wreath
on its shining nail
and since my friendly friar himself
is now long gone
to his own long home
I bow to such unchallengeably
concrete proof
of mother nature's vagaries
and shuffle credulously off

To-do
for Tina

The door is in bits
fix it forthwith
eggshells and light
to make weight

Such a high and dry
pass between quarters
you walked through me
like rain

You can't trust that stair
tread it
with feathers with scum
underfoot

The king
must go up now
his desolate angels
have gone

The gate slams abandoned
tether it tie it
with sand with great care
against strangers

Hand and tongue
can undo
what hard days and dark glamour
have joined

The bridge is back-broken
so splint it
with girders of salt and with laughter
at tides

Along thoroughfares
closed for repair
we knew ghosts to go hungry
saw the halt waters walk

The causeway comes round
again round
again round
again

leave it

Notes to the Poems

Fast Rivers: This echoes the Coplas of Jorge Manrique (c.1440-1479).

The Turlough: The turloughs or winter lakes of western Ireland occur in areas of karstic limestone. Rain falling on this land drains away through swallow-holes or sinks, but precipitation anywhere within the watershed may cause the water-table to rise again above the valley floor, whereupon streams issue through the crevices by which they had previously drained away.

The rhyme London Bridge is Falling Down is taken to refer to the ancient practice of burying alive a watchman beneath a newly-built bridge to prevent the stones being washed away.

Observation of the red shift in the spectra of distant stars revealed that the universe is expanding. If the total material in the universe exceeds a critical mass, gravity will eventually halt its expansion and the universe will implode for another big bang. Should the universe ever start to contract, this would be evident in a blue shift.

Verses with a Refrain: The specific Christ referred to bestrides the Anastasis on the paracclesion wall at Kariye Camii, Istanbul.

Lines in Fall: These take on the voice of the first two Autumn Meditations by Meng Chiao (751-814).

Orrery Hill is situated in Cork city where it rises just above Sunday's Well. It is presumably named after one of the Boyle family who were earls of Orrery. It was under the patronage of Charles Boyle, the fourth earl, that the device known as an orrery was invented. This is a mechanical model of the solar system used to demonstrate the motions of the planets around the sun.

Tenters are tenter-hooks, used for stretching cloth after manufacture. The first corporation housing estate built in Dublin is still known familiarly as 'the Tenters' because it is sited on the Tenters' Fields, which were used by the Hugenot textile-makers of Weavers' Square.

Cold Course: *As soon as the First Emperor became king of Ch'in, excavations and building had been started at Mount Li . . . They dug through three subterranean streams and poured molten copper for the outer coffin, and the tomb was filled with models of palaces, pavilions and offices, as well as fine vessels, precious stones and rarities. Artisans were ordered to fix up crossbows so that any thief breaking in would be shot. All the country's streams, the Yellow River and the Yangtse were reproduced in quicksilver and by some mechanical means made to flow into a miniature ocean. The heavenly constellations were shown above and the regions of the earth below.*
Ssu-ma Ch'ien on the First Emperor of China

Elixir poisoning was a not uncommon way of death amongst classical Chinese emperors and their courts. These elixirs were taken in the pursuit of physical immortality. Vermilion (or cinnabar), a compound of mercury, was amongst the most frequently used, and it induced ulceration, vomiting of blood, and agonising pain. Mercury excreted in the sweat or urine could often be retrieved from the sheets or mattress of the victim. Gold was also ingested for this purpose.

Coumeenole: This is the name of a strand at the western end of the Dingle peninsula, opening out onto the Atlantic from under Slea Head.

Tocharian Music: The Tocharians were an ancient people who spoke an Indo-European language and whose cities in central Asia lay on the Buddhist pilgrim route between China and India. Their rebellion against Chinese rule and the subsequent reprisal which devastated their culture occurred in the mid-seventh century. Wandering throughout Asia, their famous dancers and musicians continued after the ruin of these kingdoms to influence the greatest period of Chinese poetry and music during the T'ang dynasty. Written scores of their own music have come down to us, but lacking the necessary indications of tempi.

Cry Help: This is worked from the Irish of Aogán O'Rathaille (c.1675-1729).

Chimaera: Both this poem and The Turlough each deploy certain features of the Japanese renga form, which uses systematic ambiguity to chain together a series of brief stanzas every one of which hinges both forward and backward. This form was often used in Japan for joint composition by several poets. Chimaera is such a composite, for three voices, plaiting the disparate ghosts of Richard Lovelace (1618-57), Aloysius Bertrand (1807-41), and the original author and later interpolators of the Book of Lieh Tze. There is interference on all channels.

Tohu-bohu: Thunder Perfect Mind is one of the volumes comprising the Gnostic library found under the sands at Nag Hammadi.

The final section incorporates a number of technical terms used in computer networking.

A niptic cat would share the watchful qualities exemplified by the Niptic Fathers of the Philokalia, a collection of texts written during the fourth to fifteenth centuries by spiritual masters of the Orthodox Christian tradition.

'93/4: Algol is a binary star in the constellation Perseus in which it was often taken to represent the head of Medusa. The name derives from the Arabic Al Ghul, the demon or mischief-maker, as it was understood to be the most baleful star in the heavens. ALGOL was the first procedural computer language.

Art Ó Laoghaire, whose murder on May 4th., 1773, is mourned in the fine lament attributed to his widow, lies buried in Kilcrea Abbey, some fifteen miles west of Cork.

Emily Dickinson (1830-86), American poet.

Dogen Kigen (1200-53), Japanese poet, philosopher and founder of Soto Zen.

Federico García Lorca (1899-1936), Spanish poet and playwright.

T'ao Ch'ien (c.365-427), Chinese poet and gardener.

The immense monument of Borobodur, in Java, contains the images of many buddhas. Those near the base are clearly visible in the open while those at the penultimate level as one ascends the world-mountain are almost hidden in great bell-shaped lattices of stone, or stupas. The single stupa which stands at the highest point is completely closed, and inside it was found by its restorers an image of the buddha, whose rudimentary unfinished form is generally taken to indicate the only partial presence in our realm of a supreme buddha.

The great Hindu god, Indra, carried a net as part of his divine kit. Every intersection of this net was marked by a jewel, each of which simultaneously reflected all the others, so that the entirety was fully there at each point, though from a different perspective. The image of the Jewel Net of Indra was often used in Buddhism to indicate the essential connectedness of things, and their consequent emptiness when taken in isolation.

Golden Master: In software development, Golden Master is the ultimate stage of the code, when all testing is finished, all changes are incorporated, and all known bugs have been eliminated. At this point, version numbers are set to the final release numbers, and the disks are duplicated, archived, and sent to manufacturing.

In Greek mythology, King Midas could only rid himself from the divine gift of having everything he touched turn to gold by bathing in the river Pactolus, whose sands have ever since been thick with gold dust.

Hearsay: The burial vaults and Norman tower are part of St. Michan's church. The friary referred to is St. Mary of the Angels. Both are located in Church St., Dublin.